I0187705

# DEATH:  LIFE IN TIME

Poems and cover art were created by Desaree Masters

Edited by Colton Masters

First printed edition 2020

Masters Publishing LLC cmasters@masterspublishing.org

# DEATH: LIFE IN TIME

# DEDICATION

This book is dedicated to the people and events that inspired these poems…and to all you other people.

# CONTENTS

# DEATH:  LIFE IN TIME

## ACKNOWLEDGMENTS

I would like to thank my husband, Colton, for showing me unwavering love and support, and tolerating hot showers, which he compares to lava. Sharing your most intimate and private thoughts can be unsettling and none of this would have been possible without him.

I would like to thank my dad, Scott, for helping me develop coping strategies for life's challenges. I will never forget all the times we would take the dog for a walk and talk about everything from school and work to relationships and the future. You provided a safe place for me to grow and taught me how to step back from a problem and find new ways to solve them or deal with them.

143

# DEPRESSION/SUICIDE

## SAND IN THE GLASS

the sand in the glass has finally run dry
life must go on, and
so this is goodbye

the world will be seen through different eyes
when I'm part of the land and
the sand in the glass has finally run dry

Silence calls to me though I don't know why
and takes my hand
so this is goodbye

pale and cold 'neath the tree where I lie
under Nature's command
the sand in the glass has finally run dry

family and friends, things money can't buy
now take a stand
so this is goodbye

they pass one by one with tears and a sigh
reading the words on the stone left behind, and
the sand in the glass has finally run dry
so this is goodbye

## IF I DIE

if I die, if I never wake
these last few words I hope you take
it was my choice, it was mine alone
though many of you told me no
life is not what is seems to be
it's cold and harsh, it's not a place for me
I'm tired of the pain, the hurt, lack of joy
tired of life playing games, being coy
I'm tired of money being all that we need
instead of family and friends, life's all about greed
school's just a joke, a place to drink and get high
work is just a place to make money, to get by
It's not about trying, or how much work you put in
cause with a little money and beauty, you're bound to get in

being a kid is all about fun,
being an adult means you cannot run
people don't want average, they want a little edge, want unique
so I won't use a knife and let me life be critiqued
people want to be seen on a pedestal up high
so I'll toss in the rope and the chair for another time
the top of a building I could take a leap
but over my bloody body I don't want you to weep
Why take a pill? Why go out so cliché?
Why not stick around to see another day?

people say it gets better, but for me it gets worse,
life is a blessing and yet the biggest curse
why does it matter if I die now or years later?
I'm not afraid of the afterlife, the gods, or the creator
so if I die, if I never wake
I made my choice, it was mine to make

## WHISKEY TEARS

holding this bottle that's more than half gone
couldn't feel anything at all
I couldn't cry, couldn't laugh, couldn't smile
and then the waves began to fall

whiskey tears came pouring down
as I cried and fell to the ground
why'd you leave me, why'd you go
I'm not strong enough, no longer whole

without you there is no me
yet here I stand, I still can breath
they ask how are you? I'm doing fine.
it's the same old question, the same big lie

whiskey tears came pouring down
drunk off the pain and starting to drown
just one more sip then it's you and me
from this hell I'm in, I can finally be free
Jameson, Jim, Johnny, or Jack
grab the bottle and throw it back

## DECISIONS

when the moon is brightest, the world is darkest
confusion arises, the pain is sharpest
families are torn, loves ones are lost
the news always bad, there's always a cost

decisions are made without any thought
lessons are learned the hard way or not
the phone always rings with panic and cries
wishing and praying that a loved one won't die

closing one's eyes refusing to see
the harm that is done when emotions are set free
priorities forgotten, weeds of hate begin to grow
when all is said and done people reap what they sow

we carry a brand of the life we have chosen
the mark can be seen though the skin is not broken

## EXPLANATION

if I made you sad for leaving me here
I'm sorry, I didn't intend it
and if somehow I broke your heart
I'll do my best to mend it
you say I seem so distant now
I admit I feel it too
but all the troubling thoughts I have
are not ones caused by you
it's the stresses of life that have me down
it's theses troubles I cannot shake
and the fear of disappointing you
is a chance I cannot take
you seem so strong, unwilling to bend
I wish I could be more like you
you give me strength when I am weak
and show me dreams can come true
it's a new life I lead with no safety net
the future is mine alone
I can't turn back, I've come so far
I fear life now that I'm grown
failure haunts me and paves the way
for all this irrational fear
just know I love you more than life itself
and if not I'll try to make it more clear
there's no one else I could ever love
no one as amazing or special as you
and if I'm not making you happy enough
just tell me what else I can do
I'd do anything for you

## REFLECTION

there is comfort in solitude but also despair
for the thoughts in our head can be a living nightmare
death and suicide or reflection on life
finding the purpose or picking a knife
philosophical devotion to understanding one's self
and most of all caring about no one else
existing in a cold flame of the fire of life
how do we define death and what about life
cause while we may be living we are dead inside
so we take some pills or fight or lie
husks of a person walk around in disguise
and no one ever sees the painful tears or pleading cries

## TRUST

put down the needle, put down the knife
don't be afraid to live your life
a noose would take your breath away
that gun you'd never see another day
those pills won't ease the pain you feel
to know you're alive is to know what's real
to open your eyes and finally see
you're still standing, from the pain you're free
all it takes is one person's love
to find yourself, to not give up
put down the pills, put down the gun
it's okay to trust, to rely on someone

BLEEDING TEARS

bleeding tears of hopeless sorrow
consumed with despair
don't know how I'll get through tomorrow

another life I wish I could borrow
in the dark sitting there
bleeding tears of hopeless sorrow

Death at the ready, always waiting for the morrow
he says eternity he'll share
don't know how I'll get through tomorrow

while Death sits there smoking a Claro
my wounds are bare
bleeding tears of hopeless sorrow

I ask Death to leave, for more time I will borrow
he whispers and smiles beware
don't know how I'll get through tomorrow

in my hand, a bouquet of yarrow
sitting in a chair
bleeding tears of hopeless sorrow
don't know how I'll get through tomorrow

## LONG AGO I MADE A DEAL

long ago I made a deal,
something to live by
to always hide how I feel

even though the pain was real,
I did not cry
long ago I made a deal

I knew my heart would never heal
and that is why I try
to always hide how I feel

my true emotions I conceal
my mind, not my heart I rely
long ago I made a deal

sometimes it all seems unreal
if I have to I'll lie
to always hide how I feel

on the ground I kneel
and remind myself why
long ago I made a deal
to always hide how I feel

## TRUTH

Truth holds me down
and opens my eyes
won't let me go
no one hears my cries

I've been blind for so long
wouldn't listen to Truth's whispers
now Realization cuts me deeper
and down my spine I feel shivers

in Truth's powerful grasp
I'm pulled along
as it points out mistakes
and all that's gone wrong

to my grave I am dragged
kicking and screaming
trying to break free of the grasp
still hoping I'm dreaming

the ground still untouched
the stone not engraved
Death steps in front of Truth
and claims today's not the day

with new eyes I thank Death
for setting me free
from the pain and the sorrow
of things I didn't wish to see

Death smiles and laughs
says today's not your day
never again ignore Truth
or with me you will lay

## DESPERATION

desperation calls out like a shriek in the night
a rope ends it and the thought takes flight
withdrawing into darkness not knowing what's ahead
is it better to live life or to live life like I'm dead
the fear starts to subside as the blindness sets in
can't see past the obstacles, can't stand to breathe them in
wanting to be rescued but wouldn't mind the burning end
to feel the rapture of release, to feel happiness once again
not trusting those who matter for what's built might slowly fall
the person I was thought to be is not who they thought at all
looking deep into their eyes and trying to find an escape
reaching inside my mind and seeing thoughts take shape
the flames of stress consume me, the ashes falling down
pieces of who I was are broken and on the ground
dreaming of the troubles and not sleeping through the night
haunted by the seasons of work and social life
destroyed by expectation, hopes, and memories
until all that remains are anger, fear, and pleas

## THE CHASE

Chasing after distraction trying to satiate our desires,
but a little is never enough and to ourselves we're only liars.

Is happiness possible and, if so, what does it mean?
How can I achieve the impossible and escape the same routine?

Freedom from worry, from doubt, and frustration
in that single moment from depression we awaken.

These distractions call out to us like sirens in the night
and we chart our course as our thoughts unite.

But when we are pulled in a million directions
we analyze our life and consider defection.

The chase is the only thing that keeps us alive
the illusion of happiness that gives us our drive.

## LETTING GO

worlds in my mind created, explored
sometimes refuge and others no escape
dreaming by night or dreaming by day
traversing the maze, my mind in disarray

Darkness takes hold of all that's in sight
drowning by the weight of the lie "I'm alright"
accepting that no one can feel what I know
closing my eyes I'm ready to let go

every candle burns bright, the question is for how long
I want to fade out though I know it is wrong
so cut my wick and set me free
Death I'm waiting here please come to me

REPRESSED

alone and lost I feel depressed
can't catch my dreams
I am repressed

the cold world weighs heavy on my chest
it always seems
alone and lost I feel depressed

to those in power I'm second best
on the losing teams
I am repressed

every thought and action another test
failure or success are the only themes
alone and lost I feel depressed

unfamiliar, I feel like a guest
going through life's never-ending, failing quest
alone and lost I feel depressed
I am repressed

## WEEPING EYES

dry those weeping eyes pouring out the pain
you've held it in for far too long and with it all the shame
too proud to ask for help, yet unknowingly needing a hand
too lazy to make a change, just wishing for sailboats and sand
weighed with decisions, doubts, and regrets
in life clocks move forward, no rewinds and no resets

## DREAM

I think I'm growing weary
as this night is dark and dreary
so alas I head to bed
and hope for sleep endearing
but should I wake in earnest
with a dream of unpleasant taste
I'll return and recount the tale
and I'll do so in good haste

## TIME IS A SHOVEL

Time is a shovel that digs the grave for all
it cares not for wishes, desires, hopes, and dreams
it cares not for the pain, the hurt, the greed
for every tick of the hand the hole grows deep
it cannot choose when we lay down for eternal sleep

## THOUGHTS

my thoughts, my mind is lost in space
descending the reaches of the farthest place
time slows down as those thoughts race faster
and when I think I should act
I realize it doesn't matter
caught in the moment
you wonder what's quicker
the thoughts in your mind
or the words spoken after
the words are pulled back
to the black hole inside
no sound can escape
can't be forced, can't be pried

## MONEY

when money's put first
there's always a cost
opportunities are passed
happiness is lost
the days run together
the headaches get stronger
time slows down and
the months grow longer
inside you are screaming
but you put on a smile
and remind yourself again
that this money's worthwhile
the words that are spoken
at times feel unkind
and the looks that you get
make you feel like you're blind
you feel like quitting but
that's not who you are
and you convince yourself again
that money will take you far
but the longer you wait
and more comfortable you become
you realize your worth
and to the drama you grow numb
you look to your friends
you look to your family
you look to your true love
and realize money won't make you happy

## A DAY TO FORGET

what happens when you make a mistake
a mistake that can make your whole world break
you hurt the one you love the most
his heart bleeds when you are close
the thoughts and memories won't subside
you lay in bed helpless, alone, and you cry
giving anything to take his pain away
knowing there's nothing you can do or say
the pain is real, the pain is deep
like nothing you ever felt, feeling incomplete
when you think things are good it's only a mask
a movie or song can take you back in the past
you know things are different, so much has changed
but it doesn't matter when because the pain hurts the same
there's kind words and promises it'll be okay
but you fear what you deserve and hold your breath each day

## METAMORPHOSIS

suffocating in my own skin, constricting my very being
I keep on moving trying to break free

slowly I emerge from my shell
leaving the best and worst parts of me behind

with each new experience growing and changing
it's unavoidable, remnants of who I was is all that will remain

each ecdysis even more painful than the last
never happy with the person I am or want to be

my dreams are haunted by the thing I fear I've become
a serpent in the world with a venomous bite
cold blooded and evil to the core

## BE STRONG

I don't know what to do, and there's no where I can run
it's time to face the truth, this fake charade is done
there's so much left to learn, so much I want to see
but something always holds me back
it always comes down to money
I always try real hard but somehow I always fall
life is not a Christmas card, it's a giant concrete wall

work hard and you'll succeed, I learned that was a lie
cause you're standing on your feet, instead of learning how to fly
life is just a test, can we stand the test of time
just hold on to what you have, be strong and you'll survive

I think I'm in the clear, then find myself caught in the dark
sometimes I wish it all would end, wish I wasn't born at all
the pressure of it all is more than I can take
and soon you will realize that there is just no escape
torn between what's right,
and what you want most of all
you have to choose against your heart
even though the pain is strong

# LOVE/LUST

## I SEE THE MOONLIGHT

like a candle in the night
giving off a small spark
through your eyes I see the moonlight

in rare moments I see the fire ignite
though I know you are drowning in the dark
like a candle in the night

self-conscious thoughts you feel are a parasite
and despite your pessimistic remarks
through your eyes I see the moonlight

you say you don't want to fight
from this life you want to disembark
like a candle in the night

desperately I need insight
but your face is expressionless, stark
through your eyes I see the moonlight

I want to end your plight
in my life you've left a ripple mark
like a candle in the night
through your eyes I see the moonlight

## BITTERSWEET

how bittersweet to love
sometimes fulfilling and others unrequited
to feel connected to a person
and yet never united

to know there is no future
just a complex situation
you can love a person deeply
for a moment or the duration

no escape from hidden truths
maybe truths are only lies
when reading posts and media
or the story in your eyes

dreaming of a secret life
a parallel with you
then dismissing it as nonsense
realizing it won't be true

but the love is deeply rooted
some would say it's overgrown
because I'm not supposed to love you
but without you I feel alone

## SIN

a sin of the worst kind, a kind in my mind
have I crossed a line? But the line is undefined
I'm inclined to leave all these thoughts behind
but how can I let go of something so refined

a hidden desire to experience more
it's a chore to hide lust when I'm pressed to the floor
to you am I a bore, one you adore, or a whore
when your body touches mine is it something you ignore

curiosity holds me in a tight grip
how far will you go, will your hand ever slip
your ambiguous actions lead me on a guilt trip
if our actions are sinful closer to hell we both slip

analyzing every single move that you make
trying to understand why next to you I shake
why you're on my mind when asleep or awake
trying to figure out how these feelings I can slake

if our actions are innocent in both of our views
then why try and hide behind an excuse
when a door opens and we create a ruse
is it fear of discovery, is there something to lose

in physics we learn about energy and forces
I bet no one ever considered physics in divorces
opposites attract or are there other sources
how can I stop these feelings that he reinforces

DIPOLE

you're body pressed tight against mine
my pulse rising as you bend my spine
senses heightened and out of control
the thoughts in my head are like a dipole

innocent touch or is it much more
when you grab my wrists and pin me to the floor
we smile and laugh as I'm twisting and turning
the scuffle is growing more frequent more yearning

we move through the rooms the battleground growing
determination and temptation overflowing
when it's done euphoric thoughts endure
as much as I try I can't escape your allure

## DESIRE AND TEMPTATION

Desire and Temptation
always take the lead
to unforgettable nights
or the worst things unforeseen
Desire is always there
waiting to be found
Temptation takes your hand
and to the deed you're always bound
for one single moment
happiness is in your hand
to give in would be weakness
but against it can you stand
Desire and Temptation
always take the lead
so will you always remember this night
or do a dirty deed

## SECRETS

secrets I can't tell you
you'd rather I not say
and yet I contemplate this thought
every night and every day
I hate to keep it from you
but I fear the end result
I don't know if we'll stay friends
or if you'll want to bolt
you have your own confusion
my words could make it worse
and so I'll try to hold it back
be it blessing or a curse
would it really matter
if I said what's on my mind
or would you treat me different
would you leave me behind
would I be real selfish
would I be unfair
the thought of what might happen
or what you'll think I cannot bare
and so I'll only tell you
if you really wanna know
I'll wait for you to ask me
and if not you'll never know
secrets I can't tell you
you'd rather I not say
but maybe the time will come
a different time, a different day

## TO FEEL

to feel craved, to feel desired
to feel wanted and admired
not this fear of growing farther
time together getting harder
to feel passion, to feel love
not tossed aside when tired of
to see hunger in your eyes
but instead it slowly dies
the feelings of attraction
I feel will disappear
and the compliments you give
are growing less and less sincere
to feel anything but doubt
I want most of all
because who knows what would happen
if we can't get up after we fall

## LOSING A FRIEND

what does it mean to lose a friend
it's sorrow in your soul
and not knowing how you fucked it up
can really take its toll
was it talking on the phone too loud
or coming on too strong
analyzing every word or act
trying to decide how it all went wrong
to see you leave the room in haste
by me simply walking in
you'll never understand that pain
and the fear that lies within
the private moments that we shared
will never be forgot
even though the fruit of this relationship
has slowly turned to rot
I want to have the old you back
the one who pinned me to the floor
though I know you don't care about me
I miss the you that pretended more

## DISTANCE

absence makes the heart grow fonder
my greatest fear is yours will wander
the calls will soon blend in to one
the time spent apart can't be undone
without words we would lay together
so silence was bliss in your arms forever
but over the phone is never the same
it's awkward and quiet and silence is pain
missing your touch, your body close to me
my head on your chest, listening to you breathe
a call every night just isn't the same
the loneliness without you is the greatest pain
I'll wait for you and hope you'll see
though times will be tough I'll never flee
I'll do what it takes to keep you forever
cause I feel free and alive when we're together
I lay here in bed and try not to be afraid
that distance will make your love for me fade
should this happen and my fears come true
know I'll always be waiting and will always love you

## HOW CAN YOU FALL IN LOVE

how can you fall in love
with someone you barely know
and when you're with that person
those feelings only grow
the world doesn't spin
the sun never fades
and you want to be with that person
every minute of every day
it's not about their money
their appearance or their size
it's how they smile at you
and the love that's in their eyes
they always make you smile
they always make you laugh
when they hold you close in bed
or lightly kiss your hand
the first one in the morning
the last before you sleep
the only one on your mind
and can make your heat skip a beat
how can you fall in love
with someone you barely know
it's easy when you think of
everything this short time has shown

## MY HEART CALLS FOR YOU

feeling like a dream
my heart calls for you
everyday feeling lost cause
I never want to lose you
when you're not by my side
I lay in bed without sleep
walls around my head and heart fall apart
because you're my everything

sharp daggers of pain from a heart of sorrow
red swollen eyes wishing I could see you tomorrow
the warmth of your flesh to be felt another day
my sunny sky once bright is now gray
every phone call I wish could be longer
my love for you only getting stronger
at the end of the day, feeling alone
wearing your shirt and thinking of home

just one more text before I sleep
just one more sign our love is deep
if I dream do not wake me
I feel closer to you
cause that feeling of closeness
is often far and few
until I can leave this hell that grasps me
for your picture, your voice, your love I will plea

## ENGAGEMENT RING

an engagement ring means more to me
than just a piece of gold
it's a symbol of the love we share
and memories that will unfold
it's the promise of a happy life
the greatest guarantee
a euphoric beginning that started with
you proposing on one knee

a wedding ring means you found the one
you can't live without
and when I say the words I DO
I say them free of doubt
you're my wild card you're my blue rose
you're the happiness in my life
in white I stand before you
soon to be your wife

## WAITING

I'll wait for you as long as it takes
because I know you are the one
and though I beg for a ring
it's mostly in good fun
on ocean tides and foreign lands
adventure lies in wait
for you and I to explore the world
and together choose our fate

## SO MUCH I WANNA SAY

so much I want say, don't know where to begin
I feel like I've betrayed you, when you tried to let me in
you told me of your love, and how she did you wrong
you say that you want her back, that your love for her is strong

you shared your deepest thoughts, your crazy memories
your hopes for the future, you said this all with ease
you told me you felt shitty, I tried to lend an ear
but my mind was somewhere else, so I didn't calm your fears

it wasn't that I didn't care, that's not the case at all
but I let it get to personal, I saw one side instead of all
I didn't know how to help you or put your thoughts to rest
and I know I said some things that added to your stress

I can't take back what's said, can't make you forgive me
I don't know what you want, and what you really need
I wish things could be simple, and yet they're so complex
I wish things could be clear, but it's nothing but a mess

fear keeps me silent, I can't lie or tell the truth
if I say too much, too less, then there's more confusion for you
when the time is right, I'll try to say it all
maybe while we study or play some basketball

I'm afraid that things will change, that I'll lose you as a friend
and all the good times that we have will come to an end

## TAKING BACK

I'm living in the future and past
not the present I've sentenced myself as an outcast
to the joy and peace of the moment
always searching for the lane that's fast
but I'm taking my life back
and you may be my contrast
the question is will my feelings for you outlast
the torment you cause with unanswered questions asked
and I know you're no good for me and I hate the fact that this love
is steadfast
and tonight I'm letting you recast
better yet don't, so I can be free at last

a fictitious man you're nothing but an empty shell
the best parts of you are rotting in hell
you're dead to the world that's why from your mouth lies expel
trying to impress and find ways to compel
but it's time for me to say farewell
I can't be caught up in your carousel
going round and round I feel so unwell
cause thoughts of you hang on in my mind they dwell
and I hate to admit it but for you I fell
and it's just as well but I'm breaking the spell
I'm taking back my life and your control I will quell

## GOODBYE

I think about all the good times we had
all those memories keep flooding back
on the four wheeler in the pouring rain
or when you took me by the waist on the trampoline
and then there was prom
we had our very first kiss
or when you'd walk me home from school
all those days I will miss
swimming in the pool or movies with friends
I wouldn't trade it all for anything
but I want you to know this

you turned your back on me after all this time
you used to say I love you now you're saying goodbye
you said we'd always be friends, now I can see that's a lie
you treat me like I don't exist and I'm here wondering why
you used to care for me, I saw it in your eyes
now I'm standing alone, cause you left my side
I don't know what to do, I feel like part of me died
and I still can't believe it, but I guess this is goodbye

it's hard to believe that not too long ago
you would look at me and your eyes would glow
you put me on your shoulders and we both fell
along with everything else we swore not to tell
you used to tell me a joke, make me laugh, make me smile, you used
to call me every night, our conversations were wild
holding your hand or watching movies on the couch
and I will never forget those days
but there's something I just have to say....

## LET YOU GO

it was a little hard to breathe when you finally told me
you didn't want to be together anymore
I couldn't let anyone see how I was feeling underneath
all the heartache, tears, and questions evermore
I thought I could be strong, I thought without you I'd move on
and now I'm sitting here alone, I have no one, I'm on my own

I want to let you go
I'm searching for the answers I need to know
I want to get over you
it's time to move on but I don't know what to do
and I try not to think of you
but it's harder than I thought, I'm trying to start out new
and now all that's left to know
is how to move on, how to let you go

I have no more tears left to cry and I can finally say goodbye
I am much stronger than I ever was before
I let the heart you gave me die, replaced it with a better guy
I finally pushed you out and shut and locked the door
there's nothing you can say, I'm gonna live life my own way
and I will stand up and you'll see, you never had the best of me

I finally let you go
I found all the answers I needed to know
I can get over you
I know how to move on and live a life without you
and sometimes I think of you
how my life has changed with better things to do
and now all that's left to know
is what I wanna do and where I wanna go

## YOU SHOWED ME

ever since the day we met
I knew you were the one
I tried so hard to deny it
but your love I couldn't outrun
you're more than a dream come true
my life would be different if it wasn't for you
and I just wanted to say
with you by my side there's so much we can do

you showed me how to laugh again
you showed me how to smile
you showed me how the world could be
if I chose to stay around for a while
you took my hand and led me away
from the darkness surrounding me
you opened my eyes to the world
now I can see clearly

## ADDICTION

they tell me that I can't have you
they tell me that you're no good
I'm torn between what I want
and doin what I should
I can't get sleep at night
the way you make me feel
my hormones race inside
please take me at your will
I'm yours to command so
be rough don't be afraid
be romantic, you know I love that babe
do something different
surprise me now I wanna know
how can I please ya
cause I wanna give you more

you're an addiction baby, I can't get enough of you
you're an addiction darling, I'm cravin yeah cravin for you
like cocaine or morphine, caffeine or pot
I'll smoke you, inject you, ingest you yeah baby mmm you're so hot

I wanna give you pleasure, like you never felt before
I wanna sex ya, so shut and lock the door
you're a tease to my hormones, you make them come alive
early in the morning, or really late at night
I try to hold out, but my desire for you is strong
and I can't help it, when you kiss me and play that song
in the shower, on the bed, or on the floor
do it harder, faster baby please give me more

you're an addiction baby, I can't get enough of you
you're an addiction darling, I'm cravin yeah cravin for you
like cocaine or morphine, caffeine or pot
I'll smoke you, inject you, ingest you yeah baby mmm you're so hot

# REFLECTION/INSPIRATION

## UNDERSTANDING A DREAM

dreams they come and haunt my thoughts
for what they mean it gives me pause
to understand what's in my mind
answers to this I may never find
are dreams our secrets, our fears, and our lies
are they hopes and wishes and love that's inside
maybe dreams are not meant to be understood
and what would it mean if it ever could

## NOTHING IS AS IT SEEMS

nothing is as it seems
what's good never stays
don't get your hopes up
unless of pain you're unafraid
realization of the truth
might just set you free
but for some it only traps them
in their thoughts for eternity
is it acceptance or denial
that makes us who we are
is it knowing the path you've chosen
or not knowing where to start
nothing is as it seems
I think now I understand
if you want a broader outlook
your thoughts must expand

## DREAMING

in my mind so many questions
don't know where to begin
looking back at paths untaken
the ones I've walked and where I've been
the biggest questions are not from day
but the dreams I have at night
some leave me in confusion
others afraid or ready to fight
a dream is just a thought
but this thought was in my head
and the more I try to understand
the more I feel misled
I shake the feelings from my mind
and put a mask upon my face
until I understand the dream
or another takes its place

## ALL NIGHT

a dream keeps me up all night
it's meaning still unknown
I wish I could forget the sight

a vivid image neither black nor white
my mind is blown
a dream keeps me up all night

in the dark I search for light
in the danger zone
I wish I could forget the sight

is the dream wrong or right
is the decision mine alone
a dream keeps me up all night

over and over in my head dreams recite
My curiosity has only grown
I wish I could forget the sight

to the end I'll have to fight
to find all that can be known
a dream keeps me up all night
I wish I could forget the sight

## LONELY STREAM

I'm walking down this lonely stream
and here I'm not alone
the red, orange, and yellow fish
are swimming though it's cold
the birds are singing high above
their music oh so sweet
I listen for that special tune
so I can dance to the beat
the frogs are croaking
squirrels are jumping
and deer not far from me
so I turn around and continue
walking down this lonely stream

FOREVER

you can't hold on to forever
forever never stays
staying in the moment
a moment you don't want to fade
fading always happens
happenings shape who we are
are we only living
or living like the stars
stars are always shining
shining day and night
night brings us peace
peace shows us the light
light gives us life
life ends in death
death is forever
but nothing lasts forever

## IT MUST BE A DREAM

all the thoughts in my head are unreal it would seem
too good to be true
it must be a dream

as I move from one to the next crazy theme
so many to pursue
all the thoughts in my head are unreal it would seem

starting off simple then going to the extreme
I say it's untrue
it must be a dream

intelligent design, god's will, or my scheme
so many ideas that are new
all the thoughts in my head are unreal it would seem

impressive, original, unique, supreme
I have this new view
it must be a dream

these thoughts are not governed by any regime
they are mine alone that I must construe
all the thoughts in my head are unreal it would seem
it must be a dream

BALANCE

many fear the shadow as the dark that lies within
yet never of the balance that light and shadows give
a reflection of our self, the choices we all make
affecting things around us, building bonds or forcing breaks
shadows follow us around be it friend or be it foe

## DOWNFALL OF SOCIETY

light, light day
dark, dark night
debt and crime
war and plight
hate of life
fear of death
a world gone cold
ice hearts, white breath
disease and famine
school shootings and terror
no cure for cancer
trial and error
political parties
blaming each other
freedoms are lost
ruled by big brother
entitlement and handouts
anger and resentment
diminished middle class
growing discontentment
rallies and protesters
martial law enacted
media is deceiving
keeping viewers distracted

## WHAT IF

what if life goes on without you
what if love will never find you
what if secrets suppress you
what if lies surround you
what if dreams haunt you
what if fear captures you
what if trust abandons you
what if truth hides from you
what if beauty blinds you
what if changes pass you
what if apologies deceive you
what if death entrances you

## SEPTEMBER ELEVENTH

September eleventh
America cried
after that day
it strengthened our pride
families came closer
friends stopped their fights
some didn't care
others couldn't sleep at night
war raged on
so many died
some in the towers
others far and wide
as the years pass by
I have this one thought
do they know what we're fighting for
if asked I bet not

## TAKE THE LEAD

take the lead
a powerful stance
and see what you can achieve

stand tall, head high, and then proceed
lean how to dance
take the lead

whenever you're in need
step forward, advance
and see what you can achieve

with a little work you can succeed
put the world in a trance
take the lead

don't be caught by Greed
choose instead Romance
and see what you can achieve

you're a small seed
so take the chance
take the lead
and see what you can achieve

## I WILL SURVIVE

life will be tough and head first I will dive
sometimes alone
but I will survive

it may take some time but I'll stand and I'll thrive
cut clean to the bone
life will be tough and head first I will dive

to my death I may arrive
some fear the unknown
but I will survive

it's a gift to be alive
my life I will own
life will be tough and head first I will dive

I'll try my hardest, for greatness I'll strive
I may face a wall of stone
but I will survive

my mind and body I will not deprive
a life to live I will not postpone
life will be tough and head first I will dive
but I will survive

## WHERE I'M SUPPOSED TO BE

the wheels in my head keep turning
the thoughts in my mind never cease
the love in my heart keeps growing
the pain and the scars are at ease
the doors to my soul are locked
and I hold the only key
but the door will never open
until I know where I'm supposed to be

I can't change the past
I wouldn't want to anyway
cause everything that's happened
has made me who I am today
accept who you are and you can be free
when you understand you're where you're supposed to be

would life be different if I'd done things differently
or would different action still bring me here eventually
I don't know what life holds for me
don't know if it's choice, fate, or destiny
whether or not I like it I see
I'm exactly where I'm supposed to be

I like who I am and that's enough
I've been through a lot and times have been tough
but family and friends have been by my side
and the love of my life when I broke down and cried
it's not about actions, beliefs, or trust
it's accepting life and death, it happens, it must
everything in between is what we choose to see
I choose to see, I'm exactly where I'm supposed to be

## DESIRE AND FEAR

desire and fear both wrapped into one
trying new things, living life, having fun
knowing what you want, let nothing hold you back
facing the fear and not taking flack
be it money or time an excuse never use
sometimes life's hard but living you must choose
to dance with Death, and for Love to stop Time
no matter your age treat each day like it's your prime
do the impossible, never rush through the day
don't be afraid of losing your way
desire and fear both wrapped into one
embrace only one and Death will have won

## DREAMS

dreams are full of hope
they race across the mind
dreams show us all the wonderful things
that we think and feel inside
dreams are not the same for all
that's why they are so great
so while you're sleeping dream tonight
and dream while you're awake

## A DAY WE WILL SEE

a day will we see
with peace and love
for now only exists
a world of war and hate
separation amongst our peers
grows as we become material and selfish
both morals and love erased

a day will we see
with friendship and laughter
a time for happiness and joy
when at present time exists
only sadness and heartache
gossip and lies
deception and the loss of time

a day will we see
when money isn't everything
time will be valued
and families will be cherished
people won't be judged on possessions
but for who they are
and Death not Life will perish

a day we will see
when the time is right
when we all will live in the moment
the past behind us
the future ahead
only worrying about today
a day we will see

LIFE

it's the end of the year
a few days left to go
time to start a new life
and finally leave home
the world can be tough
don't back down just stand up
cause you can do anything if
you work hard enough

time to open your eyes
there's so much to see
stand up with your head held high
be all you can be
don't be scared you'll survive
live life to the fullest
and give everything a try
you don't know what can happen
and where life will take you next

and start a path into the unknown
don't hold back, it's time for you to grow
remember the good times and forget all the bad
live life one day at a time and never look back
now you're on your own but you're never alone
one day you will see, that we all have to spread our wings
and leave home, home, home, finally leave home

you can't live life hiding in the dark
you have to step into the light and try to make your mark

# FAMILY/FRIENDS

## R.I.P. GRANDPA

burning eyes stained with tears
looking over the pond thinking back on past years

one after another all the memories rush back
and slowly my world is consumed by black

how can I stand in this one single space
and my throat start to close and still keep a straight face

alone on this rock my eyes bleed out an ocean
as the tears pour down from this painful emotion

sunglasses on my face trying to hide swollen eyes
we're supposed to be strong when somebody dies

I stand and turn as family comes into view
pushing aside fond memories of you

but you'll always be there when I cast out a line
you'll always be there to help quiet my mind
you'll always be there

## I REMEMBER THAT DAY

I just wanted to say
though time has passed by
I remember that day

those memories float by in my head everyday
bringing a smile and a sigh
I just wanted to say

there's no fast forward, rewind, or play
those memories will never fade though I try
I remember that day

how I wished you would stay
I didn't want to say goodbye
I just wanted to say

on my mind everyday
I ask myself why
I remember that day

from the heartache I moved away
no more tears I will cry
I just wanted to say
I remember that day

## WHEN YOU LEFT MY SIDE

a part of me died
on that day
when you left my side

though I didn't want to , I cried
my world turned upside down and gray
a part of me died

I worked hard to hide
How I felt everyday
When you left my side

I knew the pain would subside
and tried not to portray
a part of me died

didn't want to break down so my hardest I tried
for my mind to take control and my heart to obey
when you left my side

I was torn apart inside
I've moved on but still say
a part of me died
when you left my side

## MAN IN MY LIFE

there's a man in my life
who's strong and smart
the sound of his voice
is as comforting as a song
there's a man in my life
who can always make me smile
if I needed him he'd come
even if a thousand miles
there's a man in my life
who taught me how to hunt
and during softball season
he taught me how to bunt
there's a man in my life
with powerful eyes
they show me he cares
and they never tell lies
there's a man in my life
who dries my tears when I'm sad
this man in my life
will always be my dad

## MIRROR

mirror, mirror hide from me
materialistic beauty
show me the woman most beautiful of all
the one who's heart is far from small
the one who loves, laughs, and smiles
and if you needed her would travel over miles
show me the one who's at every game
one who doesn't need fortune and fame
the one who wipes the tears away
calms your fears and saves the day
mirror, mirror show to me
the most beautiful woman there can be
I look in the mirror and feel so calm
the face in the mirror is my mom

## FRIENDS

friends will always be there
when life falls apart
to help you fix your problems
or show you where to start
and even when it seems
like it's only getting worse
friends will always be there
to lend an ear or converse
you may feel like there's no point
or feel like giving up
but is your glass half empty
or is it concave up
I consider you a friend
one very close to me
and I just want you to know
that your friend I'll always be
so if things get too tough
I'll try to lend a hand
Because I know we can do anything
so take the lead, you're in command

## MY TYPE

you're not my type
but you are my friend
and I hope that you
will understand
you told me that
you wanted love
but I can't give you
romantic love
you asked for something
I could give you not
cause there's someone else
I love a lot
you tell me that
I am the one
but truth be known
I'm like a gun
I kill the heart
so very fast
so that you won't
have feelings that ever last

## SICK OF IT

I'm sick of the lies, I'm sick of the fights
I'm sick of always wondering how to please you
and I don't want to be around you no more
I just can't love you anymore
how can I make you see
to my heart you brought misery

and I just want you to know
that I can't handle it anymore
and I just wanted to say
I think it's time for a change
so don't be surprised
when I tell you goodbye
it's time that I get a new life
and nothing's gonna get in my way, yeah

I'm sick of the games, and taking the blame
and now I'm trying to get on by without you
I tried to compromise, keep an open mind
but you pushed me too far and crossed the line
and now it's time to say
I think you better get of my way

## CRAZY FOOL

you drink, you smoke, do fentanyl and coke
marijuana and acid, you snort and use patches
asking for money to support your habit
shoot it up or light em up with matches

you run around like a crazy fool
always disrespectin and doin things you shouldn't do
one of these days it'll all come back on you
and you'll be alone because no one will help you

your words start slurring and your face turns real red
you throw up all the time and splash water all over your head
can't keep a job you're such a disappointment
you OD and paramedics bring you back from the dead

so much pain you can see it in their eyes
some wish you'd move away others wish you would die
you get some help and say you're gonna change
but then you'll start right back up within a couple of days

you think we're stupid, think that no one can see
you get drunk with friends and have some fun by smoking weed
you'll never grow up and you'll always be
a self-centered immature, stupid S.O.B.

three in the morning and we get a call
people wonderin where you are you're trying to outrun the law
life isn't easy and it's never fair
you can tell us bout your problems but truth is we don't care

# THE MEN IN MY LIFE

there was a time when I was young, I never knew what I'd become
but the men in my life showed me I could be whatever I want
they helped me with homework, no matter how long it would be
they took me camping, fishing, hunting, just them and me

and we were building memories, one by one
spending a lifetime of love together, always having fun
no matter how fast time may fly, or how old I may be
there will always be one thing that will remain; all of my memories

now that I'm older, I realize how lucky I've been
to have all these memories that I will never forget
each one has changed my life and made me who I am
and there are pieces in my heart of all my favorite men

and we were building memories, one by one
spending a lifetime of love together, always having fun
no matter how fast time may fly, or how old I may be
there will always be one thing that will remain; all of my memories

no matter how old I may be or how fast time may fly
there will always be one thing that will remain
and that's you were a part of my life

9 781735 363820